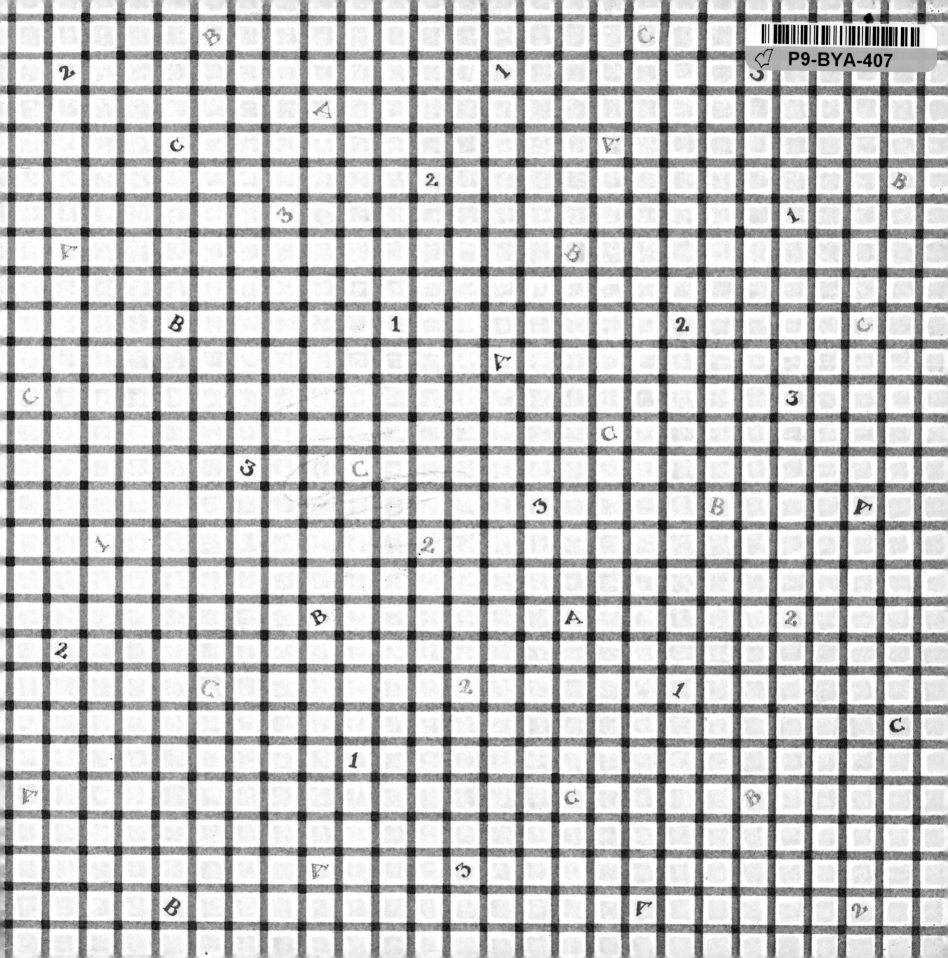

Mary Engelbreit's
Children's Companion

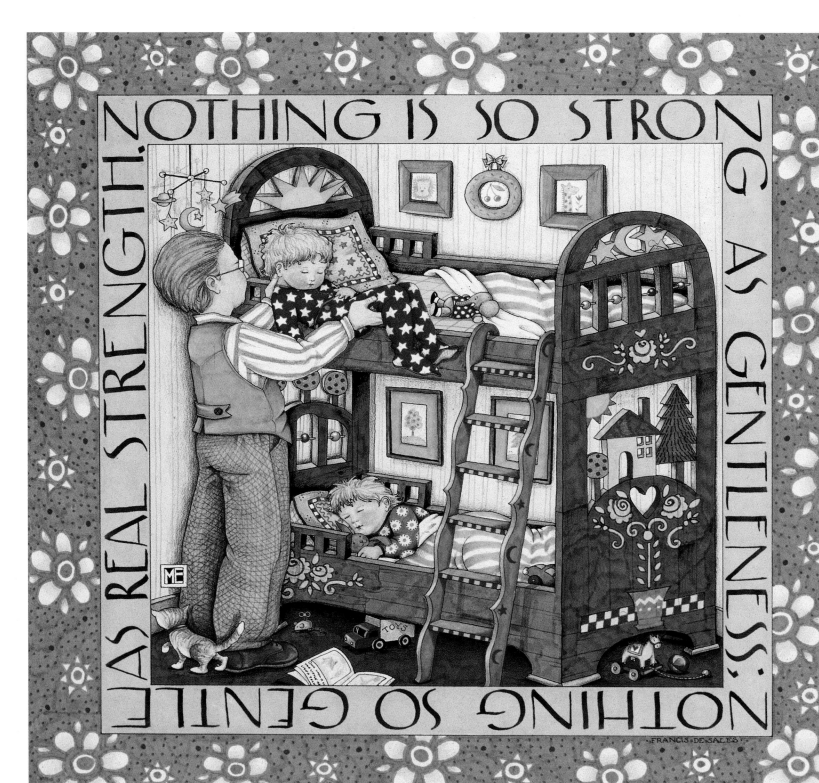

NOTHING IS SO STRONG AS GENTLENESS; NOTHING SO GENTLE AS REAL STRENGTH.

FRANCIS DE SALES

Mary Engelbreit's
Children's Companion

The Mary Engelbreit Look and How to Get It

Illustrations by Mary Engelbreit

Written by Charlotte Lyons

Photography by Barbara Elliott Martin

Andrews McMeel
Publishing

Kansas City

10 9 8 7 6 5 4 3 2 1

Library of Congress Cataloging-in-Publication Data

Engelbreit, Mary.
    Mary Engelbreit's children's companion : the Mary Engelbreit look and how to get it / illustrations by Mary Engelbreit ; written by Charlotte Lyons ; photographs by Barbara Elliott Martin.
        p.   cm.
    ISBN 0-8362-3675-0 (hc)
    1. House furnishings. 2. Interior decoration. 3. Handicraft. 4. Children's rooms. I. Lyons, Charlotte. II. Martin, Barbara Elliott. III. Title.
    TX311.E635 1997
    645' .6--dc21   97-7261
                                          CIP

Design by Stephanie Raaf

ATTENTION: SCHOOLS AND BUSINESSES
Andrews McMeel books are available at quantity discounts with bulk purchase for educational, business, or sales promotional use. For information, please write to: Special Sales Department, Andrews McMeel Publishing, 4520 Main Street, Kansas City, Missouri 64111.

Contents

Introduction

When I was a little girl, my room was my castle. My ever-patient sister, Alexa, shared it with me, but, luckily, she was perfectly willing to let me decorate. I loved spending time there—drawing, reading, and, of course, rearranging. My mother was very supportive of all this activity—even the constant redecorating, because she loved to do it, too. She respected my opinions about colors and curtains and let us hang the pictures and posters we liked where we thought they looked best. I can't tell you what this kind of confidence in my taste did for me!

Why *not* let a child help choose the colors and decorations for the one room in the house that is totally theirs? Make it a place they will want to bring their friends and a place where they can be alone. I'm not a big fan of decorating a room so that it will "grow along with the child." Who wants to stay in the same room year after year?

Kids' tastes change faster than adults. While you probably wouldn't want to change as often as my mother and I did, let your kids express themselves as they grow. The wonderful rooms in this book show a lot of different ways to create magical places for children to come home to; we hope you have as much fun looking at them as we had photographing them.

Mary Engelbreit

To our children:
Evan, Will, Erin, Maggie
Maury, Zooey, Libby

mary engelbreit

SWEET BABY

"Babies are such a nice way to start people."
— Don Herold

There are few decorating projects that receive as much enthusiasm, invention, or expense as the baby's room. Usually the nursery is a smallish space, so the project is manageable and can be as imaginative and lighthearted as possible. Some things to consider firsthand involve the business of baby: diaper changing, storage of tiny clothing and toys. Standard nursery furnishings have come a long way in handling these, but inventive solutions are all around you.

Look for unusual furniture pieces that can double as diaper cupboards—a 1930s kitchen cabinet or a Chippendale sideboard, for instance. Cover the top with an upholstered cushion and it becomes a changing table. Toys can be stashed in trunks, hatboxes, or hampers. Anything goes if it makes your baby's room a bright, warm, and well-loved place for sweet dreams. Include a rocker, a daybed, or a hammock, if you prefer. Be sure to make the walls lively to look at—with framed storybook illustrations, wildflowers painted right onto the wall, or a collection of dolly dresses strung on a clothesline—for your sake as well as the baby's; this room is for both of you. Enjoy the process—and congratulations!

Annie's Room

Annie's Chinese heritage is the focus of a collection
of charms and paper stickers above the dresser (opposite).
A garage-sale shelf with a scalloped border
has been decorated with lots of little glued-on trinkets.
Mother's collection of vintage toys from her own childhood days
is mixed in here and there.

Sunny shades of yellow and blue mix with stenciling and vintage linens to create a natural meadow feeling in this nursery. Careful attention to details created with paint keeps the space free of clutter yet full of character.

Anastasia's Room

Real linens held by clothespins tacked to the wall
"hang" from painted clotheslines (below).
Each cloth is embroidered with a different day of the week.
New nursery furniture designed in a vintage style
creates a nostalgic look.

Fresh splashes of blue and white brighten the
vintage shades found in the older linens (above).

At the window, an actual clothesline
completes the decorative theme and holds hanky-sized squares
of fabric for a light valance across adjustable blinds (right).
The fluttering birds are wood cutouts
that act as finials on the wall.

An old kitchen cupboard cabinet takes a turn as a dresser.
All the little doors and drawers do a splendid job holding mini-dresses and baby things.
Redecorated children's chairs culled from garage sales make sure everyone has a place to sit at teatime.

Aria's Room

Although her new room
called for a fresh coat of paint,
it is the randomly scattered field flowers
that provide the most excitement (left).
Garage-sale curtains and artwork
rendered by friends
are colorful points of interest.
Someday, young Aria may help her parents
choose a slipcover for her chair,
but currently, a vintage curtain panel
creates a homey quick-change throw.

A speckled clay pot holds
a bouquet of baby socks (right).

A light-filled nursery is full of family mementos that will delight young Sydney as she grows to learn their histories. She will surely appreciate her mother's own baby dress, framed and hung proudly over the crib. The toys that Sydney's father made for her sit beside those made for him by his father.

Sydney's Room

A plain toy box painted with pastel checks
takes ball feet and bows for a little personal style (below).

Vintage finds such as the switch plate (below)
complement other details
like the framed baby photograph—
a favorite outtake from picture day (above).

In a house where all the furnishings are from the Arts and Crafts period, the nursery is in keeping with that style, too.
A stencil developed just for Calli rims the room and trims the coverlet with a delicate Arts and Crafts motif.

Calli's Room

A diminutive dresser and reproduction sconce
extend the look (below).
On the door, a sweetly decorated towel bar
comes in handy for little hangers and dresses.

Framed book illustrations from the period are
favorites of Calli's (opposite), as are the silhouetted
birds enclosing
the ceiling light (above).

It's a challenge to share a room with a sister, but when she is a baby, too, it's a test for everyone.
Lacy curtains and a small-print wallpaper combine for a romantic secret garden
room where space and toys are shared in the spirit of sisterhood.

sweet baby

Courtney & Carly's Room

Favorite dresses are too pretty to hide away in the closet (below).

A mailbox attached to the coat stand
is a playful spot to stash just about anything (below).

Paris's Room

Someday, Paris Reine's mother hopes to have the time to create a border around the room with the travel-themed rubber stamps she has collected (below). For now, they fill a small shelf with other natural wood accents. The folding frame cleverly repeats the baby's first artistic impression— her footprint from the hospital.

Her parents traveled the globe
before her arrival,
so it's not surprising that their fascination
with planes continues in her nursery,
where small models
adorn the curtain rods (opposite).
A talented fabric artisan
crafted the lovely window treatments from
muslin and other dyed cottons.
The decorative trim continues on the crib
accessories and quilt.

Carson's Room

A folk art canvas embellishes a brick wall,
while a pottery lamp adorns a dresser (below).
A few strong fabric patterns
give the room energy and excitement
without overdoing it.

In an older city townhouse, a tandem bedroom presented itself
as the best spot for baby Carson (above).
When he is older he may move down the hall to a big room of his own,
but for starters, this was the perfect solution.
A colorful drapery dresses the brick doorway off the master bedroom,
and gold and scarlet fabrics bring dramatic style
to the nursery annex.

Made with Love

Decorated Toy Box

Materials:
- Unfinished wood toy box
- Rubber stamps
- Colored pencils
- Acrylic sealer and foam brushes

How To:
Use the rubber stamps to randomly scatter images all over the trunk. Use as many different images as possible and stamp them as close to each other as you wish. If you like, mark off a panel or border to decorate with a repeat pattern of alternating stamps. This will make for smaller areas between the borders that are easier to cover. After stamping, allow the stamps to dry thoroughly. Color the shapes with colored pencils in the colors of your choice. Seal the finished work by applying two or three coats of nontoxic acrylic sealer with the foam brushes.

"When the first baby laughed for the first time,
the laugh broke into a thousand pieces
and they all went skipping about,
and that was the beginning of fairies."
—James Matthew Barrie

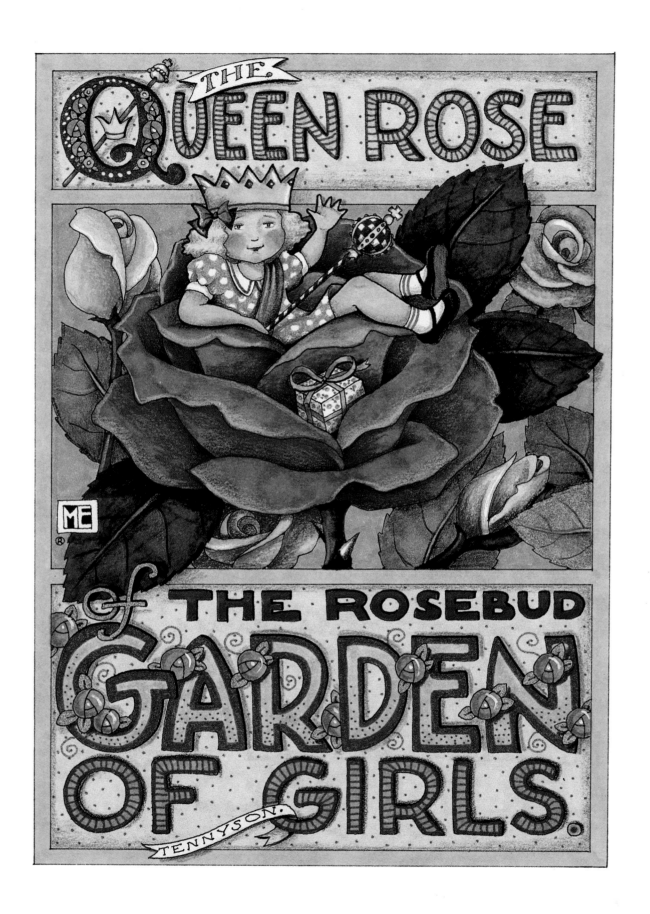

GARDEN OF GIRLS

"Little girls are the nicest things that happen to people."
—Allan Beck

Whether your daughter is a fairy-tale princess or a soccer all-star, she needs a space that gives her the freedom to express herself. Once your daughter has outgrown the nursery, be sure to let her in on the new project. Her cleverness may provide direction, and she will be much happier with the end result if she has had a hand in it. It is, after all, her room.

Girls tend to have lots of little things. Small shelves can be filled with miniatures, little postcards, or drawings. Old suitcases make great storage or display spaces.

A desk area that will accommodate a computer at some point is a sensible consideration, along with good lighting for study and reading. Built-in bookshelves can be combined with a window seat for a private retreat that becomes a sanctuary for reading—or dreaming. Wall and window treatments that will accommodate all the changes in style yet to come are a good idea, so stay open to the possibility of another redo—just for the fun of it.

Rhonda's Room

A combination of storage elements blends into a corner
with the help of a small-print wallpaper and carpet (opposite).
Vintage baby clothes and stuffed toys
add charm and character to the space.

New construction steps back in time with carefully chosen colors and accessories. Cornflower blue and snowdrop white
complement the fresh-picked colors of summer in Grandma's patchwork quilt and chenille bedspread.
A wicker armchair set beside a hand-painted table suggests a casual country spirit.

Nora's Room

A plant stand does just fine as a dressing table.
Learning to use available furnishings in inventive ways
provides the most fun in a child's room—
or any room, for that matter.

An attic dormer is a treetop bedroom with lots of cozy little nooks.
Twin iron beds leave room for a doll-sized wicker rocker and woven rag rug.
Lisa's well-loved rabbit, now past his prime, cuddles up beside a buddy bear.
Flecked with rosebuds, the wallpaper covers the ceiling and somewhat diminishes
the room's angles and imperfections.

Lisa's Room

A low window
lets in just enough light
for reading on the chaise lounge (right).
The view of the treetops
through the crocheted shawl has
inspired many a dreamy diary entry.
When Lisa went to college,
she helped her mother arrange
favorite toys on a rustic bookshelf
where they, too, can look out the window.

A fabric skirt and a glass top turns an ordinary table
into a scrapbook where a collage of
pictures and memories resides beneath the glass (left).
The perfect-fit shuttered mirror was a flea-market find.
Oh, happy day!

Big windows attract lots of attention with indoor shutters and valances made from a vintage tablecloth.
The gray-green walls are a soothing contrast to the sunny brightness.
Artwork by both mother and daughter is scattered among the crisp, white furnishings.

Eva's Room

Eva's doll collection and her mother's collages
add personal sentiment and charm (above).

Brother Cody rearranged the china animals
on the faux tablecloth side table so often that Eva finally
just glued them into place (below).
Fool the eye, then the hand.

The colorful yo-yo coverlet plays against the découpaged screen divider
to give the feeling of a Pollyanna boudoir just right for reading, paper dolls, or dress-ups.

Ashley's Room

Ashley's treasures combine easily with
her grandmother's collectibles on an antique dresser (above).

Like a Victorian dollhouse, every detail has been attended to
in this bedroom sanctuary (above).
Special toys, lacy pillows, and straw bonnets are
some of the thoughtful touches found throughout.

·ANN ESTELLE·

An old-fashioned iron bed and a down comforter create a comfortable retreat for a teenager.
Unwilling to give up the animal friends from her younger years, Lauren nestled them into the cupboard above her bed.
Bitten with the collecting bug, she has lots of new finds to mix in wherever she can.

Lauren's Room

A shallow sill works well as a shelf for
favorite postcards (left).

A dish towel makes do
as a dresser scarf for an arrangement
of collectibles (below).
Doll plates hold tiny trinkets and jewelry.

Mary Katherine's Room

Fit for a princess,
this cupboard headboard makes the most
of illusion and function (opposite).
Paired with a dressy chandelier,
it is perfect for parent and child—
toys put away and sweet dreams for all.

A sock monkey-prince keeps watch over the kingdom
from the center parapet (above).
Plastic jewels and fringed tassels adorn a crystal chandelier.

garden of girls

Hayley's Room

Balloon shades are cinched with a cluster of fabric stars (below).
Hayley and her brothers each have bird feeders
hung at their reading window seats.

Starry nights and sunny days make this room
a dreamy getaway for Hayley (opposite).
Walls painted with a blue wash are detailed
with little stars, a motif repeated on the radiator cover
as cutouts, which allow heat to escape.
Country checks stenciled at the window
echo her mother's handmade quilts on the bed.
Adding charm to the room, the peg rail
is a clever way to decorate the walls with textiles.

Alexandra's Room

Curtains are simply fashioned
from streamer lengths of ribbon (below).
Privacy is created with glass windows
sandblasted over a lace pattern.

A partitioned, hand-painted mirror reflects a pristine study in white (above).
Nursery toys still keep favor with the mistress of this serene bedroom.

Sonja's Room

Lauren's Room

A captain's bed fits neatly beneath the eaves (below). Besides the fun of this unusual berth, the added storage is always appreciated in a child's room.

In a cozy bedroom, flea-market finds create an atmosphere of romantic country comfort (above).
An old chenille spread makes a quick canopy over an iron bed, helping to soften the dark, wood-paneled walls and low ceiling.

Zooey & Libby's Rooms

Across the hall, sister Libby's room
borrowed the same elements
of style and comfort for a new look, too (below).

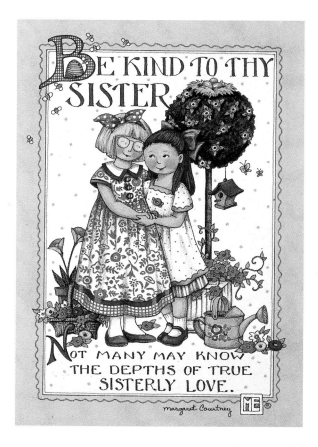

BE KIND TO THY SISTER

NOT MANY MAY KNOW
THE DEPTHS OF TRUE
SISTERLY LOVE.

margaret courtney

When Zooey entered high school,
her room needed a higher education
as well (opposite).
Updating it with a new color wash
on the walls and a ceiling-high shelf
to showcase trophies and dolls,
the room took on a new sophistication.
A recycled kitchen counter
stands in for an executive's desk,
and new plaid linens smarten the bed.
Dad's Cub Scout shirt, framed over the bed,
is both awesomely cool and dearly nostalgic.

47

Vintage gas station numbers
now signify the year of graduation
rather than the price per gallon (left).
Easily framed with a custom-cut mat,
this bulletin board holds
a collage of magazine clips.
Department-store file accessories organize
schoolwork and photos.

A pair of shutters from the garage
are perched on a bench against the wall
for another set of pin-ups (above).

Made with Love

Découpaged Makeup Tray

Materials:
- A glass pedestal cake plate
- Magazine cutouts
- Decorative tissue paper
- Vinyl wallpaper paste
- Foam brush
- Mod Podge® sealer
- Scissors

How To:

Begin with a clean cake plate. On the top arrange cutouts as you wish. It's not necessary to cover the entire surface because the tissue will be a background to cover the blank spaces. Set aside the cutouts. Trace the top of the cake plate onto the tissue. Determine the center of the circle, cut a straight line to the center, and cut away a hole for the pedestal. Repeat this procedure for the pedestal base. All the découpage will be applied under the glass so that it shows through the top of the glass. Apply the wallpaper paste with the foam brush to the front side of each cutout, and apply these face-up to the bottom side of the cake plate. Arrange while still wet to reproduce the design you planned. Press out any air bubbles for a clean seal. When dry, apply paste to the surface of the tissue backing and apply face-up to the collage. Allow to dry thoroughly and then repeat for the pedestal base. Use the Mod Podge® to apply a protective sealer to the work. This can be wiped clean but cannot be submerged in water.

"We are shaped and fashioned by what we love."

—Goethe

WE HAVE BEEN FRIENDS TOGETHER IN SUNSHINE AND IN SHADE

CAROLINE NORTON

NO GIRLS ALLOWED

"Boys will be boys."

Boys will tell you they don't much care what you do to their rooms—that is, until you do something they hate. Then you will hear all about what they really want, because they do have ideas and considerations, and they're worth listening to. Your son will appreciate being part of the project—either as a consultant or as a director. Perhaps that collection of trailside rocks or sonic robots can become an overall theme for the room or, at least, the focus of a wall or shelf. Artwork and posters in keeping with his interests are good choices for decorating the walls.

Look for ways to use detailed accents like curtain rods made from branches, a lamp based on an old ship model, or a trunk decoupaged with antique treasure maps. Built-in bunks, loft beds, or computer desks are delightful additions, especially when they include ladders, cutouts, or doors for hideouts. Like anyone else, boys like to hang out in their rooms, so comfortable seating and big drawers or bins for toys should be included, along with a worktable for building models or other projects. Sensible plans for the room embellished with imaginative touches will make a spot for your son that inspires his dreams—and yours.

A MAN AMONG MEN

David's Room

Determination, talent, and homemade whimsy capitalize on simple ingredients in this country bedroom (opposite). Painted headboards sawed from plywood panels playfully team up with assorted comforters from the blanket chest. The lamp was a weekend experiment—backyard twigs, accents from around the house, and a scrap skirt for the shade—that was fun to make and is more fun to come home to.

Evan's Room

Black tubular and formica furnishings bring a casual, mod style
to the sitting area, where toys now become part of collections
to carry into adulthood (below).
A calendar of robots in action became a framed series
above the daybed.

Evan's heavenly robot collection
meets at the window ledge as though awaiting
a starship docking (above).

Daring cherry-red walls are surprisingly restful
even when accented with bright gingham and bold checks (opposite).
The built-in bed has a carefully angled headboard
just right for reading or stargazing.

WILDERMUTH

Justin's Room

Justin's interest in magic has become a hobby and freelance career already (below).
Props and tricks are near at hand.
Curtain rods are made from old golf clubs dropped onto standard brackets.

Vintage posters of legendary magicians
fill the dark green walls
with inspiration and nostalgia (opposite).

Andy's Room

Blue and white stripes and sails set the theme
for other nautical accents.
Seashore souvenirs and vintage finds
mix together with storybooks and toy boats (below).

Tin containers make excellent storage
for sea glass, shells, and other little treasures (below).

A seaside cabana makes a clubhouse retreat for a boy
whose days at the beach start and finish here (opposite).
Board shelves from the hardware store go up in a flash
and add immeasurable possibilities to whitewashed walls.

A collage of relics found in the backyard
and around the world
assembled in a corner of the room (below).

As our sons grow older, their boyhood toys
still come out to play from time to time (opposite).
Desert colors and ethnic-patterned textiles create
a sophisticated space, and there is
plenty of room for playtime on the floor or daybed.

WiLL'S RooM

A. THE MOTHER B. ALIEN TEENAGERS

THIS TOO SHALL PASS

Bringing to mind a camp-out in the woods, Jordan's room is a serene and restful retreat
with paint and fabrics in muted woodland shades.
The rustic bed crafted from pine logs is warmed with a postage-stamp quilt and flannel log-cabin coverlet.

no girls allowed

Jordan's Room

A wonderful mix of textiles (right)!

Jordan's grandfather made custom curtain rods and brackets from branches in the backyard (above).

Joseph's Room

Jordan's Room

An elevated built-in bed is set off by
a painted checkered floor (below).
The ladder adds some adventurous pleasure to
the special refuge at the window, while
drawers and bookshelves keep everything in its place.

This close-quartered bunk room takes its cue
from the berthing compartments on a ship (above).
The crisp, nautical look reflects the captain's choice
of red, white, and blue bed coverings.
Drawers beneath the bunks are a smart use of space.

Cody's Room

An indoor awning is a fun addition to a spirited setting
filled with race cars and
high-octane colors (below).
The toy box painted by Cody's mom stands in as a
bedside table at day's end, when toys have been tucked away.

Ross's Room

A plain white box of a room is transformed
by paint patterns and jungle-jazzed linens (above).
Hand-painted stripes, rickrack, and dots create a *Goodnight Moon*
playscape for frames, toys, and accessories.
A closet door is decorated like a page out of a board book
with brightly colored shapes, while a plywood valance draws a
stage curtain over the bed. In this room, the scattered toys look
like part of the plan.

Tim's Room

Travis's Room

A computer desk with plenty of drawer
and shelf space is a boon to kids with
lots of stuff and schoolwork to stash away (below).
The wildly patterned rug is a forgiving friend
that mercifully hides spills and stains.

Though he is away at college, Tim's tailored pinstripe bedroom
is ready and waiting for his return (above).
A stack of old suitcases keeps odds and ends tucked away,
yet accessible anytime.
The rustic Old Hickory chair is nicely paired with a desktop
loaded with frames, collections, and trophies.
Unmatched blankets add a flair that identical ones can't.

Made with Love

Bulletin Board

Materials:
- Bulletin board
- Mat board
- Stickers or cutouts
- Sealer and foam brush
- Glue

How To:

Measure the inside dimensions of a framed bulletin board. Cut a piece of mat board with a three-inch reveal to fit inside the frame snugly on the cork. Arrange the stickers or cutouts as you wish in a random pattern on the mat, using the small ones to fill in the spaces between the larger ones. With a foam brush, paint on a sealer to keep the mat protected. All that's left is to glue the mat to the cork and hang.

"Youth comes but once in a lifetime."
—Longfellow

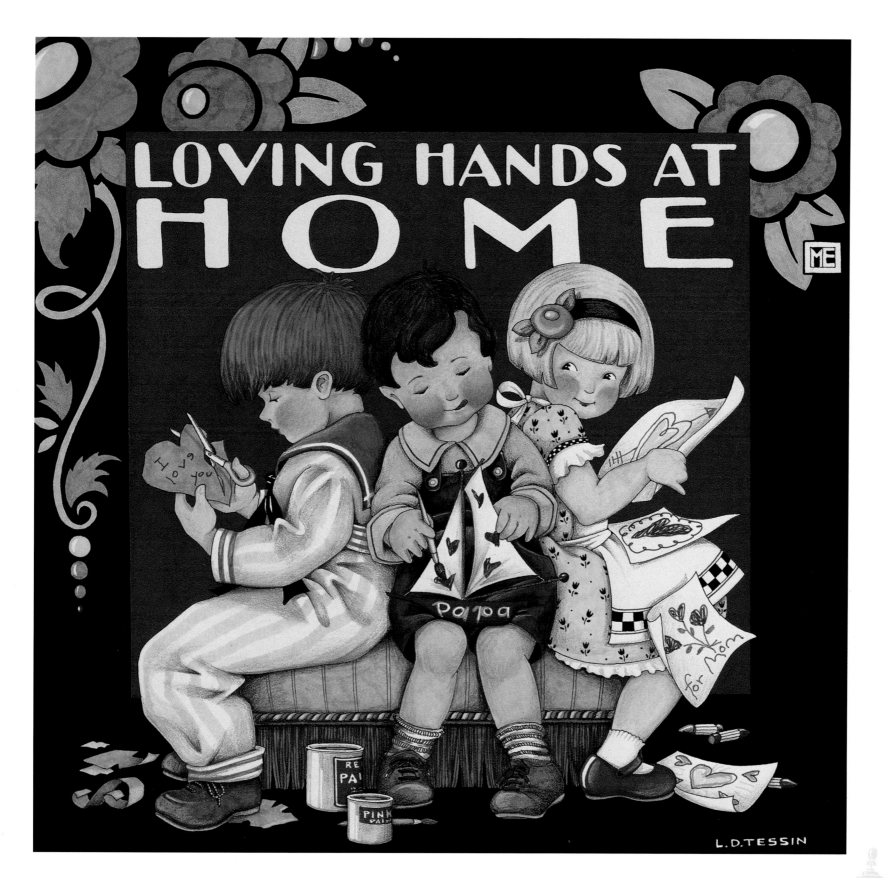

LOVING HANDS

*"I found the best way to give advice to your children
is to find out what they want and then advise them to do it."*
—Harry Truman

ost of the projects in our books are pretty easy to do. In fact, a kid could make most of them. That's because we've been watching our talented, industrious children make the most of what's at hand—and, of course, also because we don't have time for much more. With this in mind, there are lots of simple decorating and crafts projects offered in this chapter that will enliven a child's room—or make an endearing memento meant for someone special.

The best and the brightest results don't have to be the most difficult. Just look around for materials that lend themselves to decoration or recycling and then get out the glue, paints, and brushes. Make a lamp out of an old trophy cup and a crafts-store lamp kit. And then top it with a plain shade dotted with athletic achievement buttons or black-and-white photos of sports heroes. Perhaps a funky suitcase decoupaged with stickers or cutouts of ponies will corral that plastic herd of runaways. Encourage your child to try some of these ideas for his or her own room. If you're lucky, you'll be the winning recipient of the amazing creation underway.

■ ■ ■ ■ ■ ■

Look what you can do with one of Mom's glass plates
(be sure to ask her first) (opposite).
Acrylic enamel paints are permanent
when you follow the directions on the bottle
and then bake the finished project in the oven.
Eight-year-old Maury painted her pink house
onto the back of the plate so it shows through the top.

loving hands

Have some fun with papier-mâché
when you make this art caddy from a tissue box (opposite).
Cut off the top and use another box
(like a cereal box) to cut out a handle divider
and a base for the bottom.
Tape it all together and use newspaper strips dipped in paste
to cover all the surfaces.
When dry, you can paint it with acrylics
and a sealer for strong protection.

Erin found an old suitcase at the thrift store
and gave the drab vinyl covering a makeover
with a fresh coat of plum-colored latex house paint (above).
Freehand flowers and stripes in acrylics
finished the Cinderella transformation—just in time
for the pumpkin carriage going to college.

Sarah took the age-old Popsicle-stick frame and gave it a new twist with vintage celluloid charms glued to the corners. Strokes of crayon splash on more color and sweetness.

Charming family portraits
painted onto canvas boards
were framed inexpensively
inside thrift-shop castoffs (left).
But the real fun comes from Kate's clever
three-dimensional details added with fabric scraps,
tinsel hair, glittering smiles,
and a recycled necktie.

A dimestore acrylic frame takes a painted mat dotted with glued-on checkers
from the bottom of the toy box (right).
You could use dominoes, charms, or buttons, too.

Maggie made these quick frames for her friends—
color-themed to match their rooms (left).
A foam-core base was decoupaged
with a small print from magazine text
and then spotted with cutouts
of their favorite things and private jokes.
Just right for wallet-sized school or team pictures,
they were a big hit.

Use air-drying clay to make a *Three Bears* set of mini-teapots.
They would be a cheery little gift for Mom or Grandmother.
They love stuff like this—especially if you made it.

Keep your paints handy
and make your mark on a few glass bottles
from the department store.
They just take a second
and look mighty cute
filled with beads, perfume, or flower stems.

Decorate your dollhouse room with a teeny floorcloth
painted onto heavy artist's paper (Bristol board).
Carefully cut it out and move it in (below).

What could be quicker or cuter
than a plain white lamp shade
sprigged with blue buttons (above)?
Eva's grandma had better hide her
cherished button box.

Stitch up an eye-catching stocking
with scraps of felt and ribbon (below).
Whipstitch the *edges* together
along with a few bright patches.
Sewn-on character buttons
sprinkle a lively touch here and there.

Metal bookend brackets from the office-supply store
have been spray-painted red and then dotted
with white acrylic paint (above).
Little birdhouses painted with a colorful palette
are hot-glued into place
with twigs plucked right out of the backyard.

"Don't be afraid to take big steps.
You can't cross a chasm in
two small jumps."
—David Lloyd George

WHAT?! A PARTY!? FOR ME?!

A PARTY!?·FOR ME!?

"A good laugh is sunshine in a house."
—Thackeray

nother way to enjoy the lovable company and delight of your children is to celebrate the various holidays of the year with them. As creative consultants, they will come up with lots of wild ideas and proposals about party themes. Most of us can't fly the gang to the play-offs or arrange for a guest appearance of their favorite entertainer. Instead, use your combined imaginations to transform the backyard or attic studio into a stage for a fabulous celebration of your own making. The effort and enthusiasm will be greatly appreciated by everyone—not to mention your own joy at creating something from nearly nothing just for kicks.

This is a good chance to use toys and collectibles for their real purpose: fun and pleasure. Do remember, though, that this is supposed to be a good time for all—so don't overdo the decorations beyond everyone's capacity to enjoy the results. A crabby hostess can take the air out of everyone's balloon in a blink.

For a baby shower, Mary's collections of baby plates
and toys gathered from spots around the house
charmingly trim the table (opposite).
Storks from a nearby shelf perch at each place setting.
No need for flowers as a centerpiece—
there's color and sweetness aplenty.

Pink and blue china plates alternate place to place
for a baby-shower table setting (above).
Accented with silver baby cups, rattles, and teething rings, the table gleams
with these dear charms of childhood.
Decorations like these could be used for a first birthday party, too.

The garage seemed the perfect spot
to gear up a surprise sixteenth birthday party.
Cars of all makes and models rev the table with colorful fun.

In the shade garden,
a summer birthday celebration can be a civilized affair
with dainty tarts and linens (opposite and below).
Storybook figurines add an elegant touch
to the secret garden party.
Dolls are certainly welcome, too.

Crocheted doilies are tied to each napkin with ribboned bows (above).
Inside each is a scavenger's clue to help find a tiny doll
hidden in the garden.

A neighborhood tradition,
this Fourth of July potluck puts everyone to work.
Each child has his own guest list and a table to set as he chooses.
There's plenty of red, white, and blue to go around—
just follow Mom's example.

A bowlful of summer strawberries
sports a handful of patriotic toothpicks (above).

A surprise Halloween spread awaits a grade-school class
returning from the school parade.
Costumed guests are tricked and treated to vintage decorations
mixed in with new ones.
Collectibles gathered through the years
are put to good use, masquerading among popcorn balls,
licorice whips, and a handful of cookies.

Who is brave enough for a round of Whirl-o (above)?

A Christmas tea party for mothers and daughters is an annual event in this house.
Imagine the gasps of delight as the guests enter the scene and then must choose their teddy bear partners and places at the tables.

Made with Love

Hand-Painted Tea Set

Materials:

- A set of greenware dishes ready to glaze
- Ceramic glazes recommended by your pottery studio
- Brushes
- Pottery studio kiln

How To:

Locate a neighborhood pottery studio where you can choose a set of prefired but unglazed dishes (called "greenware"). Choose ceramic glaze colors and follow their instructions to decorate the dishes with a design of your choice. You can do this anywhere and then take the finished work back to the studio so that it can be refired in their kiln for a permanent glaze. If you can't locate a studio, you could purchase a plain tea set from a department store with a factory glaze and then decorate it with acrylic enamel paints. Just follow the instructions and bake the finished tea set in the oven for permanence. In this case, do not paint the inside of the cups or other areas that would come in contact with food.

"We've had bad luck with our kids—they've all grown up."
—Christopher Morley

COME OUT AND PLAY

"The best way to make children good is to make them happy."

—Oscar Wilde

Sometimes it takes more than the oft-heard "Go outside and play!" to really get kids out there. Of course, a special outpost all their own helps entice them to the backyard. Playhouses and forts are always fun to make and play in. Something as simple as a tepee or blanket strung on a clothesline may do the trick. There's something special about a little space all one's own—especially if it's in a private place. We love the little fantasy models of home that children have decorated themselves with artwork, make-do furnishings, and hours of play.

Having a garden to tend is a delightful project; bringing homegrown flowers and vegetables into the house creates a unique thrill for children. Dedicating any spot in your yard to them—even if it's just for a swing set or hopscotch court—will be a success. Perhaps you'll be invited to come out and play.

■ ■ ■ ■ ■ ■

A ready-made playhouse from the hardware center gets a unique, down-home country look with leftover house paint plus odds and ends scavenged from garage sales (opposite). Pinecones hanging from wire and screw eyes fastened to the roof provide the finishing touch.

There's nothing like a homemade playhouse in a far corner of the yard.
After all, everyone needs her own spot. The second-floor loft lookout is a favorite perch.

Brightly colored walls are fun to paint
and fun to play within as well.
If you don't have a patterned rug,
consider painting the floor to mimic one.

This elevated playhouse allows Mom to keep an eye
on Peter Pan and Captain Hook from her kitchen window (left).
A basket and rope carry secret messages
and occasional peanut butter-and-jelly sandwiches.

A pint-sized Victorian playhouse brings hours
of fun and frolic to Grandma and Grandpa's
shady backyard (right).

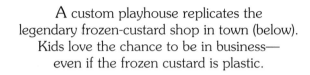

A custom playhouse replicates the legendary frozen-custard shop in town (below). Kids love the chance to be in business— even if the frozen custard is plastic.

Part of the fun of a lemonade stand is setting it up.
If you have an extra glass pitcher,
perhaps the budding entrepreneurs could decorate it
with some acrylic enamels from your paint box (below).
They should be busy until dinner, at least.

Let the neighborhood gang enjoy
a patio umbrella decorated with iron-on designs
and trims from the scrap basket (right).

Paint a set of garden pavers to create
a permanent hopscotch play spot in a shady part of the yard.
Each player gets a felt beanbag.

Customize a plain swing set
with porch finials and a funny space face
on top (above and opposite).

At the beach or in the sandbox,
sand castles are a perennial pastime (above).

IF YOU HAVE BUILT CASTLES IN THE AIR, YOUR WORK NEED NOT BE LOST; THERE IS WHERE THEY SHOULD BE. NOW PUT FOUNDATIONS UNDER THEM. ·THOREAU·

mary engelbreit

The family red wagon doubles as a portable herb garden (above).
Planted with sun and shade herbs,
it's an easy-care project for kids.
What a thrill it is to harvest daily for the dinner table.

Made with Love

Garden Scarecrow

Materials:
- Empty cans in assorted sizes, including bulk-food size
- Garden tools, watering can, and several bottlecaps
- Straw hat, silk flowers, and a bandanna
- Assorted nuts and bolts, screws, and a screw gun
- Tin snips and tin flashing strips
- Acrylic sealer and a brush

How To:
The materials you choose will call for your own solutions and invention as you go along. Be prepared to customize your project to suit whatever you have at hand. If you want the labels to last, paint them with acrylic sealer to weatherproof the paper. Wash the insides and size the cans to build the body, laying them out on the ground for the look you want. Use the screw gun to assemble the cans, carefully screwing bottoms to each other or through the sides when that works better. Use the watering can for the head and paint on a face. Flattened bottle caps make rosy cheeks (and connectors for other tough joints). Big wing nuts stand in for ears. Add

garden tools for hands or feet and drop the straw hat on top with a big sunflower on it. Wirey kitchen scrubbies make crazy hair and tin flashing strips create suspenders, if you like. A tied-on bandanna and a crafts-store crow perched on his shoulder give the scarecrow that funny farmer look.

"Self-confidence is the first requisite to great undertakings."

—Samuel Johnson

SUGAR AND SPICE

"Home is heaven for beginners."
—Charles H. Parkhurst

Children live all over a house just like their parents do. Creating welcome environments for them in all rooms makes a home suitable for everyone who lives there. One formal living room uses the sofa as a screen for a hidden toy area behind it in a bay window. Baskets of toys might sit in a row beneath a library table in the den where Mom pays the bills.

In the hallway, a cupboard can become a toy cabinet in the same way that a kitchen drawer devoted to arts and crafts supplies or games and puzzles keeps the fun near at hand. This chapter also includes smaller decorating arrangements that we discovered in odd spots around the house where tight quarters meant creative solutions. A kid-friendly house is a joy to be in—amusingly energetic and full of the unexpected.

■ ■ ■ ■ ■ ■

Dress-ups are always available on the hall tree upstairs, where hats, gloves, and purses are in full bloom (opposite).

Setting up an easel or drawing table in any room
is always a good idea (opposite).
This one fits into a corner
already full of playful muses!

A table from the basement
and an old medicine cabinet come together
for an impromptu dressing table (opposite).
It's decorated with a gathered skirt
and a collage under the glass top.
The mirrored cabinet
holds all the little things that would otherwise
clutter the tabletop.

Colorfully painted walls provide a backdrop
for a collage of keepsakes arrayed on simple shelving (above).
Poster putty holds lightweight frames and trinkets to the wall,
while papered boxes used as organizers
become display cubes as well.

An extra bedroom has been reassigned
as the computer room (opposite).
The painted-on rug and punched-tin cupboard
make this functional space
attractive, too.

Game boards on the wall
lead down the hall to a desk for homework (above and left).
The landing area is private enough for study,
but easily monitored by Mom.

The living room sports a garage-sale cupboard
tranformed with paint and paper
into a vertical toy box (opposite).
Videos, dress-ups, and toys
line up inside.

In a tandem bedroom, a trompe l'oeil open book
is painted onto the desktop (right).
The sunny study corner is abundantly welcoming
with its tropical colors, squiggley swirls on the shades,
and a mural painted by Eva and her friends.

It's Phillip's turn to spread out his favorite things
on the entry table by the front door (left).
His show-and-tell assembles
one grandfather's paint-by-numbers landscape,
the other's war medals,
and Phillip's own box of arrowheads.
Next month,
his sister Maggie will showcase her treasures here.

In a little girl's bathroom,
the sink is used to scrub doll dishes and faces (right).
Towels rolled and ready in the basket beneath the sink
are handy for all sorts of washing up—
and for spills, too.

Made with Love

Decorated Lamp Shade

Materials:

- A lamp base and shade to fit
- Rickrack trim
- Paper ribbon or decorative paper in a pattern you like
- Color photocopy of a favorite image
- Spray adhesive
- Thinned white glue

How To:

Size your image and photocopy it to fit the particular dimensions of your lamp shade. Trim around the edges of the copy carefully and apply spray adhesive to the back of the paper. Apply the image to the front of the shade, carefully smoothing it out to eliminate air bubbles. Cut out shapes from the strip of paper ribbon or decorative paper to match. These shown here are just triangles and circles. When you have enough to go around the whole shade and you have marked their placements lightly on the shade with a pencil, apply spray adhesive to a few at a time and position as planned. Glue rickrack around the top and bottom of the shade.

"Ideas won't keep: something must be done about them."
—Alfred North Whitehead

TO IMAGINE IS Everything...

TO KNOW IS NOTHING AT ALL

ANN ESTELLE'S ROOM

"A happy family is heaven on earth."

If you were a grandmother, (Ann Estelle was in real life—before she became a character in a drawing), wouldn't it be wonderful to have a room just for your grandchildren? A room full of all the dearest toys, places to play, and coverlets to snuggle up in. A room where Nonny could read, play pretend, and make up stories with each little one—a storybook nursery in the old-fashioned sense, for children of all ages.

Just for fun, Mary assembled a dream-come-true room in that very same spirit for a charity showcase house. Maybe some of these ideas will come to life in your house, if not now then sometime in the future. We hope you'll have fun with all of it. Living and playing with children is the best. Enjoy the journey.

■ ■ ■ ■ ■ ■

This room was easily big enough to take a crib and a bed,
so Mary's vintage nursery set found a home here
along with many more favorites (opposite).
A home-stitched baby coverlet is suspended with ribbon hangers
from a dowel decorated with cutout bird finials
above the elephant-footed crib.

129

Nonny's chair sits amidst a field of quick and easy decorating projects.
The turtle stool was a flea-market find repainted and covered to take on more character.
A plain lamp shade is rimmed with powder-puff balls of fringe,
and with a little imagination a folksy magazine stand becomes a story rack.
Even the quilt rack has been sprinkled with pattern and color.
Little touches like these are fun to do, and children are fascinated by the details.

ann estelle's room

Nearby, a single twin bed fluffed with pillows of all kinds is kept company by a series of nursery prints.
The toy box has been painted with polka dots and posies.
Collectibles and books are near at hand for stories at bedtime.

Mary often chooses older pieces of furniture
from shops and repaints them for fun (opposite).
She likes those that have design features
suitable to her decorating style—
spools, doors, and feet allow for a lot of detail.
This toy cabinet and dottie dresser
are typical examples of her refurbishing.

This shelf is a great way to display souvenirs
from the seashore (left).
To make your own, sketch out the sailboat shape
on newspaper and then fold it in half.
Cut the paper in two at the crease and use each side
as a template for the ship pattern.
Use a jigsaw to cut out the two shapes from plywood
as well as triangular shapes to act as shelves.
Using wood glue and nails, assemble the shelf
as shown in the photograph.
Then paint it any way you choose.

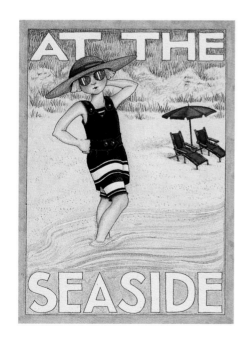

A private bathroom uses sherbet tones
to warm up chilly gray marble
with pastel dots and dishes (opposite).
The shades on the sconces wear new floppy skirts
fashioned from hankies.
The shelf just above takes its charm
from the bracket supports and scalloped trim
cleverly cut out and painted up.

The LEMONADE sign
reverses to become a POST OFFICE (left).
So many jobs to do, so little time.

The fun really begins in the closet-turned-playroom (opposite).
Taking the door off and adding a swinging gate with a sign
inspired all manner of whimsical additions.
Lattice was applied to the little window for a clever privacy screen,
and all the important business of the day can be taken care of
on the desk beneath.

What would this room be
without a dollhouse done in
Mary's unique style?
Checkered floors and
chairs of bowlies are found inside,
of course!

Credits

Sweet Baby

Annie's Room, Linda Solovic and Gary Karpinski, St. Louis, Missouri. **Anastasia's Room**, Jill and David Haack, Chicago, Illinois; *interior design: Jill Haack and Carol Schalla, Chicago, Illinois; stencils: Andreae Designs, Sterling Heights, Michigan.* **Aria's Room**, Melanie Wells, Chicago, Illinois; *painted cupboard, chairs: Melanie Wells; decorative paint treatments on walls, toy box, and chairs: Mary Joe Leverette, Oak Park, Illinois; family portraits: Kate Olivola, Oak Park, Illinois.* **Sydney's Room**, Julie and David Walker, St. Louis, Missouri. **Calli's Room**, Lauren Gabor and Scott Goldstein, Los Angeles, California; *stencil and paint treatment: Ed Pinson, Pinson•Ware, Los Angeles, California.* **Courtney and Carly's Room**, Julie and Brent Cassity, St. Louis, Missouri. **Paris Reine's Room**, Nancy Hannon and Dan Bogosh, Chicago, Illinois; *curtains and linens: Claudia Ahuile for Kachi-Bachi, Chicago, Illinois.* **Carson's Room**, Jackie James and Lloyd Schoen, Chicago, Illinois. **Decorated Toy Box**: *Linda Solovic, St. Louis, Missouri.*

Garden of Girls

Rhonda's Room, Rhonda and Doug Cassity, St. Louis, Missouri; *interior design: Sonja Willman, St. Louis, Missouri.* **Nora's Room**, Nancy and Bill Keenan, Oakbrook, Illinois; *painted table: Nancy Keenan.* **Lisa's Room**, Marie and Bill Trader, Hinsdale, Illinois. **Eva's Room**, Kathy and Michael Deitch, River Forest, Illinois; *collages, clay pots, pillow on bed: Kathy Deitch.* **Ashley's Room**, Sonja and Bob Willman, St. Louis, Missouri. **Lauren's Room**, Roberta and Dave Williamson, Cleveland, Ohio. **Mary Katherine's Room**, William and Elizabeth Joyce, Shreveport, Louisiana. **Hayley's Room**, Kathy and Rich Brooks, River Forest, Illinois; *quilts: Kathy Brooks; decorative paint treatments: Christine Baumbach, Oak Park, Illinois.* **Alexandra's Room**, Martha Young and Jock McQuilken, Atlanta, Georgia. **Lauren's Room**, Rod and Jill Perth, San Marino, California. **Sonja's Room**, Sonja and Bob Willman, St. Louis, Missouri. **Zooey's and Libby's Rooms**, Barbara and Bud Martin, St. Louis, Missouri. **Découpaged Makeup Tray**: *Charlotte Lyons, Oak Park, Illinois.*

No Girls Allowed

David's Room, Sally and David Weaver, La Grange, Illinois; *beds and lamp: Sally Weaver.*
Evan's Room, Mary Engelbreit and Phil Delano, St. Louis, Missouri. **Justin's Room**, Sonja and Bob Willman,
St. Louis, Missouri. **Andy's Room**, Mary Engelbreit and Phil Delano, St. Louis, Missouri. **Will's Room**, Mary
Engelbreit and Phil Delano, St. Louis, Missouri. **Jordan's Room**, Kathy and Rich Brooks, River Forest, Illinois;
quilts: Kathy Brooks. **Jordan's Room**, Karen and Robert McNamee, St. Louis, Missouri. **Joseph's Room**,
Becky and Louis Portera, Dallas, Texas. **Ross's Room**, Carolyn Mandernach, Des Peres, Missouri; *interior design
and paint treatments: Cindy Kuhn, St. Louis, Missouri.* **Cody's Room**, Kathy and Michael Deitch,
River Forest, Illinois; *toy box: Kathy Deitch; quilt: Kathy Brooks, River Forest, Illinois.* **Tim's Room**, Betty and
Jerry Scanlon, Burridge, Illinois. **Travis's Room**, Kathy and Rich Brooks, River Forest, Illinois.
Bulletin Board: *Charlotte Lyons, Oak Park, Illinois.*

Loving Hands

Painted plate: Maury Lyons, Oak Park, Illinois. Art caddy: Charlotte Lyons, Oak Park, Illinois.
Suitcase: Erin Lyons, Oak Park, Illinois. Popsicle frame: Sarah Bush, St. Louis, Missouri.
Family portraits: Kate Olivola, Oak Park, Illinois. Checkered frame: Cindy Kuhn, St. Louis, Missouri.
Collaged frames: Maggie Lyons, Oak Park, Illinois. Teapots: Maggie Lyons.
Painted bottles: Charlotte Lyons. Button lamp shade: Kathy Deitch, River Forest, Illinois.
Floorcloth: Kathy Deitch. Bookends: Maggie Lyons. Felt stockings: Kathy Deitch.

A Party!? For Me!?

Baby shower: Mary Engelbreit, St. Louis, Missouri. Baby shower: MarGee Farr for the Garden Collection,
Hinsdale, Illinois. Sixteenth birthday: MarGee Farr. Garden party: MarGee Farr.
Fourth of July: MarGee Farr. Halloween: Ted Frankel, Andy Needham, and Dave Vail for Uncle Fun and Flypaper,
Chicago, Illinois.
Hand-Painted Tea Set: *Sonja Willman for the Summer House, St. Louis, Missouri.*

Come Out and Play

Pinecone playhouse: Jeff and Anne O'Connor, Oak Park, Illinois.
Red playhouse: Margaret Lesher, Orinda, California. Elevated Playhouse: Cary and John McLean, Oak Park, Illinois.
Yellow playhouse: John Giege, St. Louis, Missouri. Custard shop: Carolyn Snidle, Festus, Missouri.
Lemonade stand: Joseph Slattery, St. Louis, Missouri. Hopscotch and chair: Joseph Slattery.
Sand castles: Libby Martin, St. Louis, Missouri. Swing set: William and Elizabeth Joyce, Shreveport, Louisiana.
Garden in a wagon: MarGee Farr, Hinsdale, Illinois.
Garden Scarecrow: *Joseph Slattery.*

Sugar and Spice

Dress-up hall tree: Sonja Willman, St. Louis, Missouri. Art easel: William and Elizabeth Joyce, Shreveport, Louisiana.
Dressing table: Maggie Lyons, Oak Park, Illinois. Colorful shelves: Kathy Deitch, River Forest, Illinois.
Collaged frames: Maggie Lyons. Computer room: Karen McNamee, St. Louis, Missouri.
Game boards: Mary Engelbreit, St. Louis, Missouri. Desk, shades, and mural: Kathy and Eva Deitch.
Toy cupboard: Melanie Wells, Chicago, Illinois. Show-and-tell table: Phillip and Maggie O'Connor, Oak Park, Illinois.
Bathroom: Julie Cassity, St. Louis, Missouri.
Decorated Lampshade: *Charlotte Lyons, Oak Park, Illinois.*

Ann Estelle's Room

Mary Engelbreit Studios, St. Louis, Missouri.

Grateful Acknowledgments

Dave Bari, Stephanie Barken, Cardinal Glennon Children's Hospital Designers' Show House in St. Louis, Missouri,
Kathy Curotto, MarGee Farr, Rick Hill, Jean Lowe, Ed Pinson, Stephanie Raaf,
Romantic Homes in St. Charles, Illinois, Joseph Slattery, Linda Solovic, Patricia Dreame Wilson,
and our crafty kids.

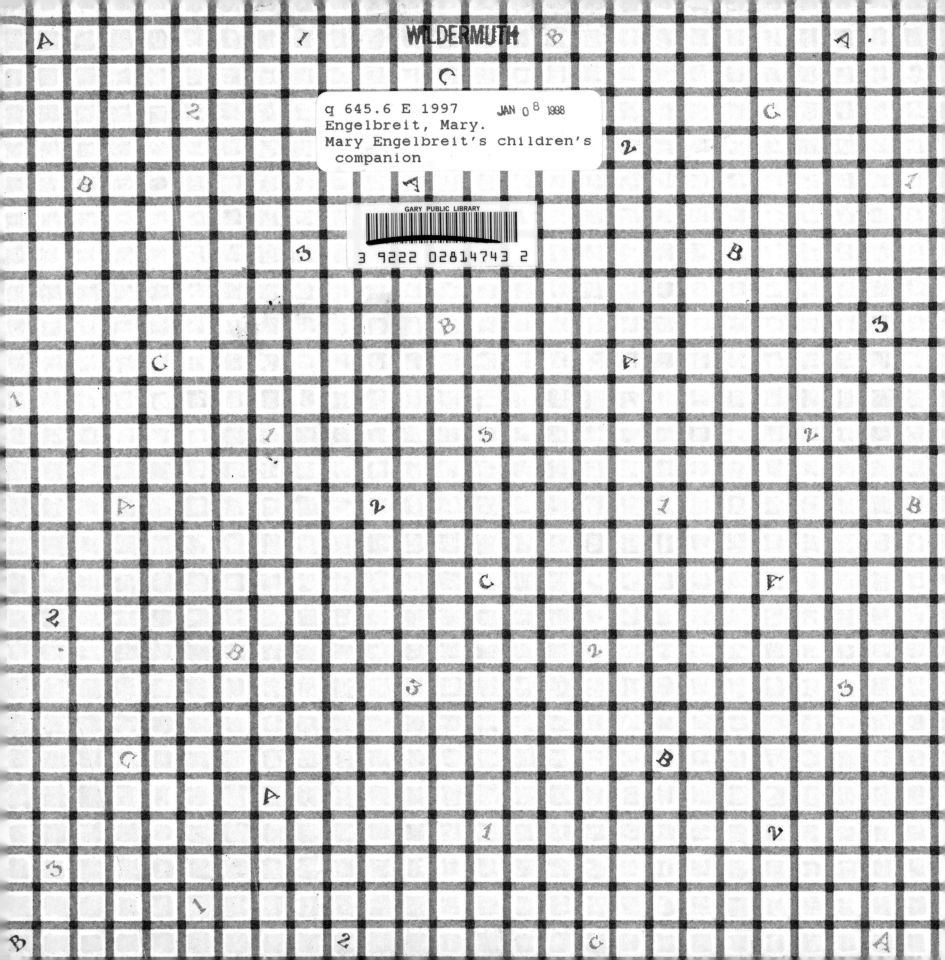